Are you ready for an Art Attack?

These scary Art Attacks will send shivers down your spine! Lurking amongst the pages you'll find some terrifically terrifying ideas for wicked things to make, featuring mean monsters, beastly bats and ghastly ghouls! Follow the step-by-step instructions and discover how to use everyday junk to create a haunted house of your very own.

So let's get spooky and make some Art Attacks!

CONTENTS

Editor: Caroline Repchuk
Designer: Joanna England
Artist: Mary Hall and Paul Gamble
Model Makers: Claire Keen
and Caroline Repchuk

Haunted House

THIS SPOOKY STORAGE BOX IS THE PERFECT PLACE TO HIDE ALL YOUR SECRET STUFF...

1 Take a cereal box and cut around the front on three sides as shown.

2 Open back the flap and fix strips of card to the front and side with masking tape to reinforce it. Tape on an extra piece of card, just slightly smaller than the front flap, for extra strength.

3 Cut two windows in each of the kitchen rolls and tape them to the front of the flap to form turrets. Cut two circles of thin card and slit from the outside edge to the centre. Twist each circle into a cone shape and tape along the slit edge. Stick the cones in position on the top of the turrets to make roofs.

4 Cover the whole box, inside and out, with two layers of black tissue paper and diluted PVA glue and leave it to dry.

NO-ONE WILL BE BRAVE ENOUGH TO PEEK INSIDE!

5

Paint your box in spooky colours as shown, adding details like the brickwork and slits for arrows. Paint the insides of the tower windows black. Cut a central window and door shape from card, paint them and stick them into position. Don't forget the ghost!

YOU WILL NEED:

A cereal box, safety scissors, two kitchen rolls, thin card, black tissue paper, masking tape, PVA glue, paints, paintbrush.

Put a little ghost in the window to scare away any snoopers!

TRICK OR TREAT?

THESE SPOOKY STORAGE JARS ARE PERFECT FOR KEEPING TREATS...

1 Plan your design before you start, thinking carefully about which colours you will use.

2 Starting with the lightest colour, completely cover the outside of the jar with a layer of tissue paper papier maché, using diluted PVA glue, and allow it to dry.

3 Draw your design onto the tissue paper with a pencil.

YOU WILL NEED:

Clean glass jars without labels, PVA glue, tissue paper, silver crêpe paper, pencil, marker pen.

THINK ABOUT HOW THE COLOURS MIGHT CHANGE WHEN YOU PLACE ONE COLOUR TISSUE PAPER ON TOP OF ANOTHER.

ART ATTACK

4 Add the next layer of tissue paper, working within the pencil lines you have drawn. Leave each layer to dry before adding the next one.

5 Finish by outlining your design with marker pen. Make a collar for the jar with silver crêpe paper, to finish it neatly. What will you put inside – something nice… or something nasty?

WANDS + BR

1
Choose two colours of paper and cut out one hundred squares – fifty of each colour. Each should be 2cm square.

2
In the centre of the coloured card mark out a grid with a ruler and pencil. The outside edge should be 24.5cm square, allowing 2cm for each square and 0.5cm for the spaces in between.

3
Carefully stick the coloured squares in position, alternating the colours.

YOU WILL NEED:
A large piece of thick coloured card, coloured paper, stick-on stars, googly eyes, PVA glue, pencil, ruler, a die.

Wands and B

Finish

100	99	98	97	96
81	82	83	84	85
80	79	78	77	76
61	62	63	64	65
60	59	58	57	56
41		43	44	45
40	39	38	37	36
21	22	23	24	25
20	19	18	17	16

Start

| 1 | 2 | 3 | 4 | 5 |

8

BROOMSTICKS

Broomsticks

95	94	93	92	91
86	87	88	89	90
	74	73	72	71
66	67	68	69	70
55	54	53		51
46	47	48	49	50
35	34	33	32	31
26	27		28	29	30
15	14	13	12	11
6	7	8	9	10

4 Cut wands and broomsticks from black and white paper and glue them on the grid in whatever position you like, making sure the edges are clearly placed on a square.

5 Finish by carefully numbering each square and adding plenty of spooky decorations cut from coloured paper, with stars, glitter and googly eyes added for extra effect. Paint the name of the game at the top.

6 For the counters, make witches' hats by cutting a small circle of black paper as a base and adding a cone of black paper for the pointy part. Stick a different coloured star on each one so you can tell them apart.

PLAY THIS GAME IN THE SAME WAY AS SNAKES AND LADDERS, GOING UP THE WANDS AND DOWN THE BROOMSTICKS!

WICKED WITCH!

FRIGHTEN YOUR FRIENDS WITH THIS MENACING MASK!

1 Fold a piece of A3 paper in half and draw half a face on it. Make it the same length as your face, with eyes and mouth marked in position. Make the chin and ears long and pointed.

2 Cut out the face template and tape it to the corner of a cardboard box. Draw around it and draw a straight line across the top. Cut it out, then cut out the eye and mouth holes.

3 Cut curvy eyelids from cardboard and glue them in position with PVA. To make warts, dip some kitchen roll in diluted PVA and squeeze out the excess, then press them onto the mask. Make a large, hooked nose from scrunched-up kitchen paper held in shape with masking tape. Tape it on to the centre of the mask.

4 Cover the whole mask with three layers of papier maché and leave it to dry.

5 Paint your mask with a coat of white paint. When it's dry, paint it in shades of green and turquoise with purple lips. Outline the eyes in black pen.

6 To make the hair, cut a large bundle of black and green wool into strands slightly longer than the mask. Cut a slot in the top of the head and push the ends of the wool through. Make sure there is enough wool to pack the slot tightly. Put some masking tape on the other side to secure it.

Ghostly Gravestone

STOP INTRUDERS IN THEIR TRACKS WITH THIS TERRIFYING TOMBSTONE DOORSTOP!

1. Partly fill an empty cereal box with small stones to make it heavy.

2. Cut a ghost shape from white card. Make sure he's the right size, so his body and arms fit behind the tombstone and his tail sticks out at the side. Carefully draw around his outline in black marker pen and add a scary face. Secure the ghost to the back of the tombstone with a paper fastener, with his face towards the box. Tape the top of the box shut.

3. Cut two semi-circular pieces of card to the same width as the box. These will form the curved top of the tombstone. Stick them to the top of the cereal box with tape.

4. Cut a strip of card to the same depth as the box and tape it across the top to both semi-circles.

5. Cover the whole thing with three layers of newspaper papier maché. Finish with a layer of black tissue paper and leave it to dry.

PRESS ON THE GHOST'S TAIL AND WATCH HIM POP OUT FROM BEHIND THE GRAVE!

6 Paint the tombstone by dabbing grey and silver paint on with a soft cloth or a stiff brush to get a stone effect. Paint the letters and ivy with a fine brush.

7 To make a base, cut a rectangle of thick card and stick a piece of greengrocer's grass, green felt or a green carpet offcut to it with PVA glue. Now you can stand your tombstone in position and use it to prop open your door!

RIP

R.I.P

RIP

You will need:

A cereal box, small stones, thin card, white card, safety scissors, masking tape, newspaper, black tissue paper, PVA glue, paint, thick cardboard, greengrocer's grass, carpet offcut or green felt.

Gruesome Ingredients

THIS MAGICAL BOX IS THE PERFECT PLACE TO STORE YOUR SECRET SPELLS!

1

Cover the shoe box with silver paper using sticky tape and set it to one side.

2

Take a piece of strong cardboard the same length as the shoebox and draw on five different shaped bottles. They should overlap each other with three at the front and two behind. Give the tops interesting shapes.

3

With a marker pen, draw around the outline at the top and outside edges. Cut around the outline carefully.

Think up some different ingredients! How about?

FROG'S LEGS

SLIPPERY SLUGS

MONSTER CLAWS

POND SLIME

HAIRY TOES

FROG SPAWN

WITCH'S WARTS

CREEPY COBWEBS

Large shoe box, strong cardboard, safety scissors, tissue paper, PVA, paint, coloured paper, silver paper, sticky tape, double-sided sticky pads.

4 Cover the shape with two layers of tissue paper papier maché and leave it to dry.

5 Paint the bottles different colours and paint magic ingredients inside each one. Use black paint to outline the bottle shapes. Make labels for each bottle from coloured paper and stick them on with PVA glue.

6 When it is dry, stick the bottle shape in place on the side of the shoe box using double-sided sticky pads.

Mice

Spiders

Eyeballs

Rat Tails

Snails

SPOOKY PARTY

SET THE MOOD FOR SOME SCARY FUN WITH THIS SPOOKY PARTY STATIONERY!

STENCILS

1 Draw the design for your stencil in pencil onto thin card and carefully cut out the shapes. You may need to ask an adult to help you. Keep your design simple or it will be too difficult to cut out.

2 Lay the stencil on the surface you want to decorate and fix it in place with masking tape.

3 Use a thick paintbrush to dab paint over the stencil in a 'stippling' motion (dotting). Don't overload your brush – remove any excess by dabbing it on some newspaper first.

4 Carefully remove the stencil by lifting one corner and peeling it away gently, taking care not to smudge the paint.

DECORATE PARTY BAGS, INVITATIONS, ENVELOPES AND DOOR SIGNS!

SPOOKY PARTY BAG

POTATO PUMPKINS

1 Ask an adult to cut a potato in half for you. Draw a pumpkin face onto the flat surface with a thin marker pen, then ask an adult to help you carve it out.

2 Coat the potato with orange paint then press down lightly on a piece of dark paper and leave to dry. Try all different shapes of potato for some funny pumpkin faces.

16

PACK!

STRING WEB

1 Glue some lengths of string onto a piece of cardboard in a web pattern and leave it to dry.

2 Carefully load the string with paint, then press down lightly on a piece of paper to make a web pattern. Now all you need are the spiders…

MAKE PARTY BAGS FROM COLOURED PAPER WITH GOLD STRING AND BEADS FOR HANDLES!

Charlie's Party Bag

CORK SPIDERS

1 Dab a cork into some black paint spread on a sponge cloth and press it on to a piece of paper.

2 When the paint is dry, draw on legs with a marker pen. Finish by sticking on googly eyes.

RATTY RACERS

SIT BACK AND ENJOY THE SCREAMS AS THESE TEARAWAY TERRORS SPEED ACROSS THE FLOOR!

1 Cut off the cup sections and pointy sections from inside an egg box. You'll need two cups and one pointy section for each rat.

2 Stick the two cups to the top of a toy car. Tape the pointy section to the front. Make sure you don't cover the wheels.

3 Tape a strip of card to the back of the rat. Add small pieces of scrunched-up newspaper to build up the body.

4 Cover the whole thing in two layers of papier mâché, avoiding the wheels, finishing with a layer of black tissue paper. Leave it to dry.

5 Finish by painting the rat, dabbing on brown paint with some kitchen paper. Add two card ears, painted pink and stuck on with PVA, and a little ball of tissue for the nose. Stick on some googly eyes.

6 Make a hole below the nose for the whiskers by pushing the tip of a sharp pencil or pen through each side (ask an adult to help with this). Cut a drinking straw into thin strips and thread them through the hole and out the other side.

& SPEEDY SPIDERS!

YOU WILL NEED:

Old toy cars, egg boxes, thin card, sticky tape, old newspapers, black tissue paper, PVA glue, paint, googly eyes, clear drinking straw, black pipe cleaners.

1 Tape four black pipe cleaners on to a toy car, bending them into leg shapes. Trim them so they do not touch the ground. Take care not to cover the wheels.

2 Tape a scrunched-up ball of newspaper over the whole car to form the body shape.

3 Cover the whole thing with two layers of papier mâché, using black tissue paper, avoiding the wheels. Leave it to dry, then stick on some googly eyes.

MONSTER

THIS SPOOKY THEATRE WILL SET THE STAGE FOR A MEGA MONSTER BASH!

1 Ask an adult to help you cut a hole in the shoe box lid 2cm in from the edge all around. Cut a slot 1cm wide in one long side of the shoe box, along the whole length, and approximately a third of the way in from the top edge.

2 Tape the lid on to the shoe box with masking tape.

3 Cover the outside of the box and lid with two layers of black tissue paper papier maché.

YOU'LL FIND LOTS OF PETRIFYING PUPPETS TO MAKE INSIDE THE BACK COVER!

20

PARTY!

4 Paint the inside of the box black.

5 Stick on twigs, arranging them to look like trees. Add googly eyes, peering out from between the branches. Paint on details like the moon with a bat flying across it and finish with some stick-on stars.

21

CREEPY CAULDRON!

SEE WHAT KIND OF TERRIFYING MONSTER
THE CAULDRON HAS COOKED UP TODAY!

1 Draw a cauldron shape with a large looped handle and two legs onto a piece of cardboard and cut it out.

2 Use this as a template to draw around and cut out another cauldron shape, but without the handle. Draw a window in the centre and cut this out.

3 Cover the cauldron shapes completely in two layers of black tissue paper pasted on with diluted PVA glue.

4 Glue the front frame to the back, making sure you only put glue across the top and halfway around the edge of the cauldron. Leave one side open so you can slot in different pictures.

5 Decorate your frame with stars and glitter. Draw a worm and a frog's leg on coloured paper, cut them out and glue them in place, so it looks like they're sticking out of the top of the cauldron.

You Will Need:

Cardboard, safety scissors, black tissue paper, PVA glue, paint, thin card.

ART ATTACK

Slot in a scary picture and abracadabra... your spell has worked!

23

GHOSTS ON GUARD

THESE CHEEKY LITTLE GHOST BOOKENDS WILL LIVEN UP YOUR BOOKSHELF!

1

Fill a plastic bottle with sand or pebbles and replace the lid.

2

Scrunch up a large ball of newspaper, big enough for a head. Find a piece of soft cloth large enough to cover it easily. Place it over the newspaper, then use a rubber band to secure it in place on top of the bottle.

YOU'RE SURE TO HAVE A WAAAAIL OF A TIME MAKING THIS ART ATTACK!

Colin Bateman

BEWITCHED IN THE BATHROOM   ROBINSON

ELEANOR UPDALE   MONTMORENCY   AND THE ASSASSINS   SCHOLASTIC PRESS

101 THINGS TO MAKE   TREASURE PRESS

Unexplained Phenomena   A ROUGH GUIDE SPECIAL

HART   CARTOON COOL   How to Draw New Retro-Style Characters

RICHARD I   John Gillingham   Book Club Associates

CHRYSALIS CHILDREN'S BOOKS

Ruth Thomson

ART ATTACK

3

Ask an adult to help you cut the pillowcase in half around the seams so you are left with two rectangles. Carefully round off the corners.

YOU WILL NEED:

Two small drink bottles, sand or pebbles, old newspaper, soft cloth, large rubber bands, an old white pillowcase, four safety pins, safety scissors, thin card, felt-tip pens.

4

Place one piece of fabric over the base. It will have two long sides and two short sides. Hold the long sides together and fasten them in position with a safety pin.

5

Draw eyes, eyebrows and a mouth onto thin card with felt-tip pens and cut them out. Stick them on with PVA to make a ghostly face!

A First Look at Art

UNDERWATER ORIGAMI THE MAGIC BOOK

The Ratbridge Chronicles VOLUME 1

HERE·BE·MONSTERS!

STEVE AND MEGUMI BIDDLE

Alan Snow

OXFORD

Jane Bull

RED FOX

APPLE FICTION #14 GIVE YOURSELF Goosebumps® ELEVATOR TO NOWHERE R.L. STINE

APPLE FICTION #8 GOOSEBUMPS THE GIRL WHO CRIED MONSTER R.L. STINE

CORGI Terry Pratchett

BAT ATTACK!

DON'T DRIVE YOURSELF BATTY TRYING TO REMEMBER STUFF, THESE BARMY BATS WILL HELP!

To Do.....
• tidy bedroom
• maths homework
• call Sarah
• birthday present for Dad

YOU WILL NEED:
Thin card, safety scissors, glue felt-tip pens, pegs, string.

ART ATTACK

Neil Buchanan

1
Photocopy the templates as many times as you like, depending on how many bats you want.

2
Stick the page on to thin card and colour in the bats.

3
Carefully cut them out and stick each one to a wooden peg painted black.

4
Tie a piece of ribbon or string up in your bedroom and then clip on your notes, invitations and reminders.